W9-BUH-204

STORY OF
HAWAII
COLORING BOOK

Y. S. Green

DOVER PUBLICATIONS, INC.
Mineola, New York

CONTENTS

Copyright

Bibliographical Note

Story of Hawaii Coloring Book is a new work, first published by Dover Publications, Inc., in 1999.

International Standard Book Number

ISBN-13: 978-0-486-40565-0
ISBN-10: 0-486-40565-6

Manufactured in the United States by Courier Corporation
40565607
www.doverpublications.com

INTRODUCTION

The islands of Hawaii were created by volcanic eruptions that pushed up lava from the ocean floor. Formed from 25 to 40 million years ago, these islands, isolated in the Pacific Ocean, were uninhabited by humans for millions of years.

Polynesians began to settle on the islands of Hawaii between approximately 500 and 800 A.D., bringing with them their rich culture as well as the necessities of life. After two waves of human migration—the first from the Marquesas, the second from Tahiti—the islands fell into isolation once again. In the following centuries, the transplanted Polynesian culture evolved into a way of life that was distinctly Hawaiian.

In 1778, isolation ended forever with the arrival of the first Westerner, Captain James Cook. Once contact with the West was established, life on the Hawaiian islands underwent dramatic changes. Explorers, traders, whalers, missionaries, and immigrants came to Hawaii, forcing the reordering of Hawaiian society.

The newcomers brought diseases that ravaged the native Hawaiian population. At the end of the first 100 years of Western contact, the demographics of the islands had shifted so dramatically that there were more outsiders than there were native Hawaiians. As a result, Hawaiians lost their beloved 'āina (land), as well as their independence. In 1898, Hawaii became a territory of the United States.

In 1959, Hawaii became the 50th state in the Union. Today, it is a true melting pot, with a mix of many ethnic groups. It has become an important center of political and economic life in the Pacific region.

KAUA'I

NI'IHAU

O'AHU

Honolulu

MOLOKA'I

LĀNA'I

Lahaina

MAUI

KAHO'OLAWE

THE HAWAIIAN ISLANDS

HAWAI'I

Polynesians. The Polynesians are believed to be people who migrated from Southeast Asia to the Pacific in about 1500 B.C. Excellent sailors and navigators, Polynesians used the sun, the stars, the wind, and the birds to discover the islands now known as Hawaii. Over a few thousand years, Polynesian voyagers, shown above, settled in each island group of the "Polynesian triangle." People from the Marquesas islands appear to have migrated to Hawaii in their double-hulled canoes between approximately 500 and 750 A.D. A second wave of Polynesians, the warlike Tahitians, are thought to have begun to settle and conquer the islands in about 1200 A.D.

1.

4.

5.

3.

2.

Native species. More than 2,000 species of plants and about 60 varieties of birds inhabited the Hawaiian islands when the first Polynesians arrived. Forerunners of these species had reached Hawaii by wind, wave, wing, or other natural forces. Over the course of a million years, species adapted and evolved into unique forms that were endemic to Hawaii. Polynesian settlers and European voyagers introduced new plants and animals that brought devastating changes to the Hawaiian ecology (see pages 8 and 9). Many of the native plants and animals, which had existed

in isolation for so long, could not survive the onslaught of the aggressive new species or the diseases that they carried(see page 24). Rare, endemic animals and plants survive in Hawaii today only in insulated, upland regions.

Shown here are the (1) *nēnē* (Hawaiian goose), (2) *'ō'ō*, (3) *'i'iwi*, (4) *pueo* (Hawaiian owl), (5) Hawaiian bat, (6) *'io* (Hawaiian hawk), (7) *'alalā* (Hawaiian crow), (8) Hawaiian monk seal.

Plants brought by the early Polynesian settlers. In their canoes, Polynesians brought the plants that were essential for their food, clothing, shelter, and general survival. They used nearly every part of a plant. Some of these plants are shown here. (1) Bananas were used for food; (2) coconuts were used for food and building materials; (3) gourds were used for containers; (4) nuts from the candlenut tree were used for candles and dyes; (5) sugar cane; (6) sweet potato, and (7) breadfruit were used for food; (8) ti plants were used for wrappers and place mats. (See page 9 for ti plants; page 14 for *taro*, a food; and page 22 for *hala*, used for mats and ornamentation.)

Animals brought by the early Polynesian settlers. Also in their voyaging canoes, Polynesians brought the pig (*pua'a*), the dog (*'īlio*), and the Polynesian chicken (*moa*) (which they raised for food and for use in religious ceremonies). The Polynesian rat (*'iole*) probably arrived in Hawaii as a stowaway. Settlers hunted the rat for sport using bows and arrows. The people in this illustration are preparing a pig and *laulau*, a kind of food wrapped in ti leaves, for a *lū'au*, or feast.

Ali'i. Under the feudal system in ancient Hawaii, each island was ruled by one or more chiefs, called the *ali'i*. High chiefs, kings, or queens known as the *ali'i nui*, sometimes ruled over several lesser *ali'i*. *Ali'i* status was determined by ancestral *mana*, or divine power. Each kingdom was organized by chiefs, priests, and warriors. Commoners paid taxes to them in the form of crops and handicrafts. It was very important to ancient Hawaiians to preserve family histories. To do this, the *ali'i* used rhythmic chants to memorize long lists of information. (See page 12 for more on rhythmic chants.) The *ali'li*, believed to be descended from God, was protected by many strict laws and taboos called *kapu* (see page 19).

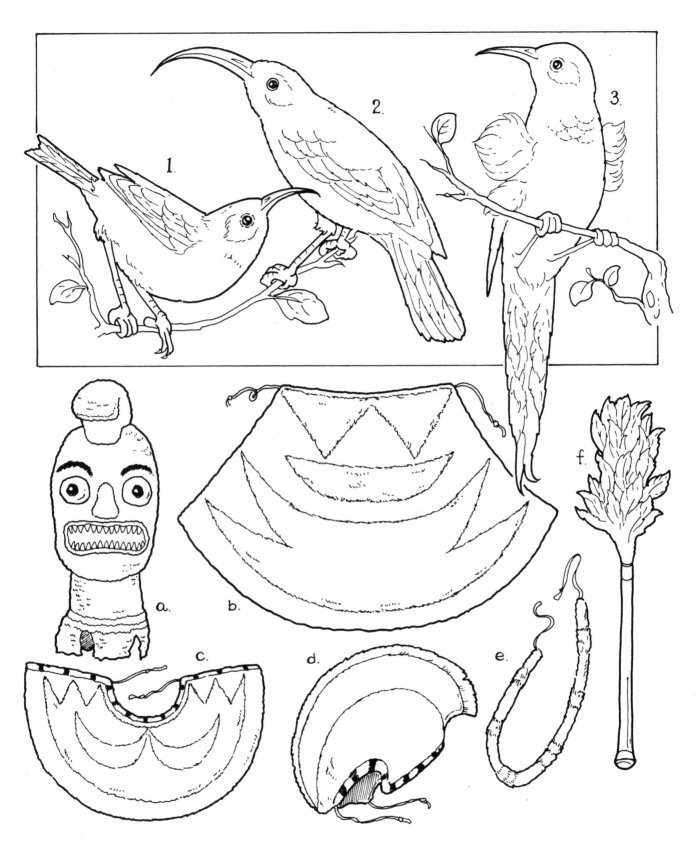

Hawaiian feather work. A designated bird catcher hunted particular native birds for materials to make feather capes and cloaks for the *ali'i*. Some of these garments were so elaborate that they may have taken up to 100 years to complete. Many of the birds whose feathers were used, such as the 'ō'ō, are now extinct. Since the color yellow was a symbol of rank and *mana*, the amount of yellow feathers used in a cape indicated the status of the *ali'i*. Only the highest ranking *ali'i* was allowed to wear an all-yellow mantle. Shown here are (1) *'i'iwi* with crimson feathers, (2) *mamo* with black feathers, (3) 'ō'ō with tufts of yellow feathers under the wings.

Also shown are (a) an idol image, (b) cloak, (c) cape, (d) helmet, (e) *lei*, (f) and *kāhili*, or royal standard.

Mele. *Mele* means song, chant, or poem. Since the ancient Hawaiians had no written language, they passed their histories down through the generations in the form of memorized oral literature called *mele*. This spoken tradition enabled generations of Hawaiians to learn their genealogies, religious traditions, legends, and philosophies, as well as to record their experiences.

Hawaiian gods. Hawaii's early settlers brought their belief in the gods of Polynesia. The four major gods were *Kāne,* the most important, the provider of sunlight and water, the creator of heaven and earth; *Kū,* god of war; *Lono,* god of peace, agriculture, and fertility; and *Kanaloa,* god of the ocean. In addition, there were countless minor gods and goddesses. Pictured here is (1) a carved god in a *heiau* or temple, as well as (2) paddlers wearing gourd masks which may have been associated with *makahiki* festivities honoring the god, *Lono.* (For more, see pages 14 and 21.)

Farming. The Hawaiians were excellent farmers who developed more than 300 varieties of taro, one of their essential foods. They prepared *poi*, a staple in their diets, by pounding taro root until it was smooth, then thinning it with water. They ate it with their fingers. The spiritual and peace loving Hawaiians worshipped *Lono*, the god of agriculture. Because they believed that all living things possessed *mana*, or divine power, they respected nature and conserved natural resources.

Fishing. Fish and seaweed, which provided protein and minerals, were also important foods for ancient Hawaiians. Fishing techniques included using nets, spears, hooks, and lines. In addition to fishing in the sea, ancient Hawaiians built a great number of fish ponds.

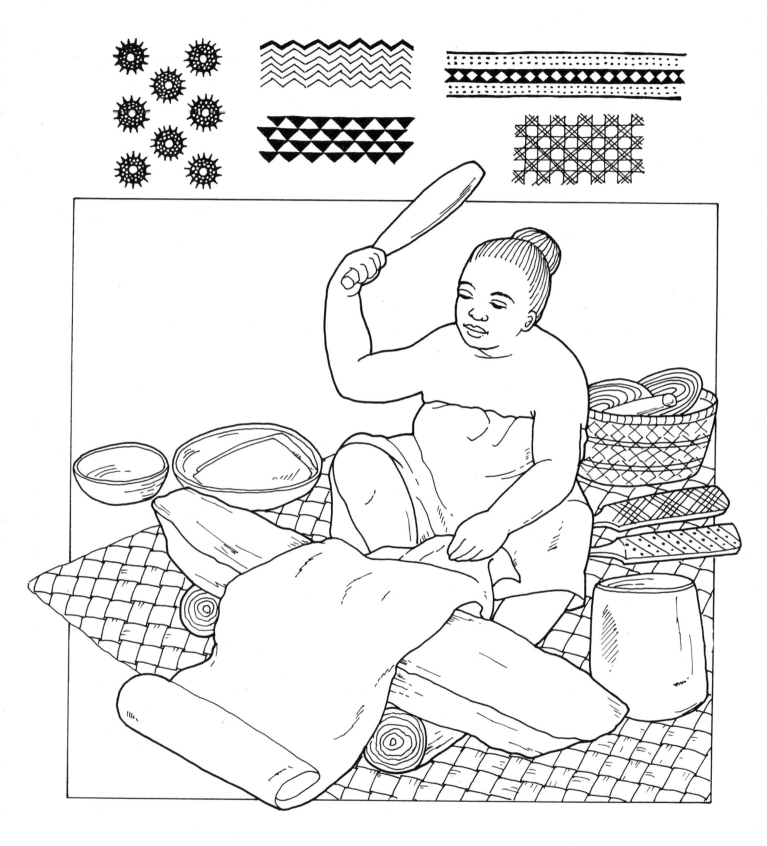

Kapa. Polynesians brought the *wauke,* or paper mulberry bush, as well as other useful plants to Hawaii. They beat and sun bleached the *wauke* to make *kapa,* also called bark cloth. *Kapa,* or tapa in English, means "the beaten thing" in Hawaiian. Although it was made by people throughout the Pacific, the *kapa* cloth made by Hawaiian women, usually dyed and stamped with colorful patterns, was revered for its design, color, and overall quality.

Clothing and shelter. Except for royalty, people of all classes wore basically the same style of clothing. Hawaii's warm, subtropical climate inspired the creation of three main garments made from *kapa*. The *malo* was the men's loin cloth; *pā'ū* was the women's skirt or sarong. The third piece, a shawl worn for warmth by both men and women, was the *kīhei*. In addition, to keep warm and dry, fishermen wore capes made from ti leaves. Most people lived along the breezy shorelines. The *hale noho*, or Hawaiian house, was a simple building covered with thatched *pili* grass and ti leaves.

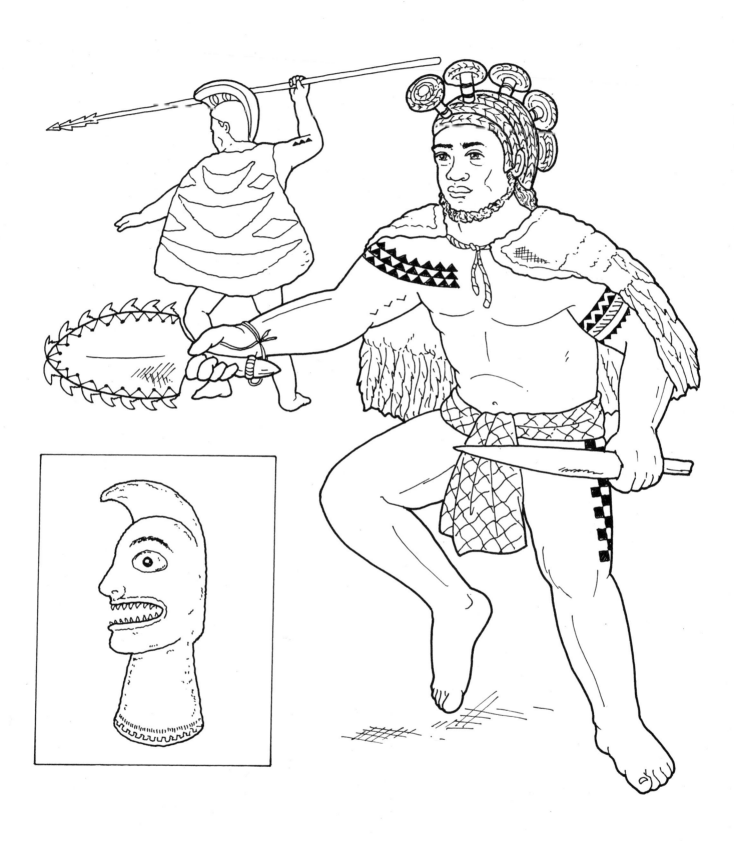

Warfare. Wars of succession were frequent. Before a battle, an *ali'i* would honor *Kū*, a war god, by ordering the construction of a large, sacred temple called *heiau*. The frequent battles brought destruction, famine, and death. Warriors wore feather capes, cloaks, and feather or wicker helmets. Their weapons included clubs, daggers, spears, and tools edged with shark teeth. Shown here is *Kūkā'ilimoku*, a war god.

Kapu. The lives of ancient Hawaiians were organized and regulated under strict laws. *Kapu* means forbidden. For example, women were not permitted to eat with men. The penalty for breaking a law was often death. However, *kapu*-breakers were provided with places of refuge. If they reached a place of safety before being caught, they could ask for sanctuary. Shown here is *puʻuhonua*, a city of refuge. Built 800 years ago, today it is a national park.

19

Hula. The *hula* is the dance of the Hawaiian people. The earliest type, the *mele hula,* or rhythmic dance chant, had two forms. One version, used to worship a god, or an *ali'i,* was danced by men in a temple. The second kind of *hula,* which was performed in public, often recounted an his-toric event, or made a social or political comment. In addition to vocal chanting, the instruments that accompanied the hula included shark skin drums, gourds, nose flutes, and bamboo rattles. The two dancers shown here wear dog teeth leglets.

Games and pastimes. The *makahiki* festival, a period when war was forbidden, was dedicated to *Lono*, the god of agriculture, and to the *ali'i*. During this time, from mid-October through mid-February, ancient Hawaiians enjoyed recreations such as sports competitions and dance.

Many chiefs encouraged men to master wrestling, spear-thrusting and throwing, as well as fencing. Surfboarding, called *he'e nalu*, originated in early Hawaii. The couple shown here is playing a quiet game similar to checkers.

Weaving. Hawaiians were among the finest basket weavers and mat makers in Polynesia. They wove *ulana,* or mats, from leaves of the *hala* tree, shown above. These mats, with intricate geometric patterns, were used as floor cov-erings, as sleeping mats, and as mats for sailing. Coconut palms, used to make braided coconut-fiber rope, called sennit or *'aha,* also provided important material for the construction of houses and weapons.

Petroglyphs. Petroglyphs are 2-dimensional images that ancient Hawaiians chipped into hard surfaces using sharp rocks. Most Hawaiian petroglyphs were incised in *pāhoe-hoe*, a smooth, unbroken type of lava. Little is known about the specific meanings of these symbols, but among the thousands that have been found, some seem to represent genealogies, battles, fishing, hunting, and games of ancient Hawaii.

Arrival of Captain Cook (1778). The two strange white, floating objects, first seen from Oahu, were British ships, the "Resolution," and the "Discovery," led by the British explorer Captain James Cook. On January 20, 1778, Cook made landfall on Kauai, the first recorded Hawaiian contact with Westerners. Because the *makahiki* festival which honored Lono was underway, native Hawaiians welcomed Cook warmly, believing that he and his crew were gods. Cook named the islands the "Sandwich Islands" in honor of his patron, the Earl of Sandwich. Returning a year later to *Kealakekua* bay (the pathway of God), Cook was killed during a brief dispute with Hawaiians.

Gifts and diseases. Captain Cook introduced goats to the Hawaiian islands in 1778. In 1794, Captain George Vancouver brought cattle and sheep as gifts for the chiefs and to ensure a food supply for himself and his crew. The populations of these animals exploded as they roamed freely throughout the islands, destroying crops and turning native forests into bare plains. The animals also carried foreign diseases which infected and killed many native animals.

Kamehameha I and united Hawaii. Under Hawaii's ancient feudal system, there were frequent wars among the *ali'i*. Kamehameha, (the "lonely one"), was a young, strong, wise, high-ranking warrior from the Big Island who fought with Western arms and vessels. By 1795, Kamehameha had established the kingdom of Hawaii; by 1810 he had brought all of the islands into his domain. Under his rule, the Hawaiian people enjoyed peace for the first time.

Missionaries (1820–1832). When Kamehameha's son came to the throne in 1819, he issued a royal decree ordering Hawaiians to give up the ancient *kapu* system and the Polynesian gods which had been central to their lives for centuries. In 1820, the first missionaries from New England arrived in Hawaii, quickly establishing new cultures and religion. The missionaries built churches and schools. Adapting the oral Hawaiian language to the English alphabet, they published newspapers and bibles, converting many Hawaiians to Christianity. Descendants of the missionaries dedicated themselves to developing plantation agriculture, commerce, and democratic government in Hawaii.

Holoku and mu'umu'u. When Christian missionaries landed in Hawaii, island women were wearing only the *kapa*, a skirt or sarong, wrapped around their bodies. Missionary women showed the chiefesses how to cut and sew loose fitting, graceful dresses that were more discreet. The new fashion, spreading quickly throughout the islands among women rich and poor, became "island dress." The earliest style of dress (1) featured long sleeves and a plain yoke. The *holoku* (2) is a fitted formal dress with a short or long train. The *mu'umu'u* (3), an everyday island dress with a yoke, is made from colorfully printed fabric. It is worn in a variety of lengths, from short to long, with short sleeves, or sleeveless.

Hawaiian quilting. New England missionaries introduced Hawaiian women to traditional American quilting. Hawaiians, long skilled in creating unique designs on bark cloth, quickly brought their own sense of style to this new technique. Cutting, folding, and stitching, they used Hawaiian motifs, inspired by island flowers and plants, to create intricate, 2-color, appliquéd quilts. These elegant Hawaiian quilts, respected as art, often became a family's prized possession.

Paniolo. Long before cowboys rode in the American West, Hawaii had cowboys called *paniolo*. In 1832, Kamehameha III brought horses and skilled riders to Hawaii from California, then part of Mexico. They taught the Hawaiians how to handle large herds of cattle, called *pipi*, which were roaming the islands. Ranching soon became a major industry in Hawaii.

Whaling (1820s–1850s). In the 1820s, when whales were plentiful, Hawaii became the whaling capital of the Pacific Ocean. This industry made Honolulu, situated on Oahu, and Lahaina, located on Maui, the busiest ports of the Pacific. During the whaling seasons, hundreds of vessels visited the islands, bringing commerce, foreign goods, and foreign diseases, until the whaling industry declined in the 1860s.

Father Damien. Because native Hawaiians had lived in isolation for so many centuries, they had no immunity to Western disease. During the first hundred years of Western contact, the Hawaiian population declined from 300,000 to 50,000 people. Leprosy, also called Hansen's Disease, appeared in Hawaii in the 1830s. Molokai was chosen as the place to confine the ill. Father Joseph Damien de Veuster, a 33 year old priest from Belgium, devoted his life to the leprosy victims there. He built a hospital and churches, established farms, and cared for patients, until he died of the disease at age 49.

King Kalakaua, the "Merry Monarch." The 7th, and last king in the Hawaiian monarchy, David Kalakaua was known far and wide as the "Merry Monarch." He was an educated, European-style ruler who enjoyed the ceremony of royalty. In his 17-year reign (1874–91) he supported the traditions of Hawaiian culture, built the second 'Iolani Palace (see page 39), and made a widely publicized world tour.

The **Hula kahiko.** Missionaries attempted to stamp out *hula* dancing and in 1830 public *hula* performances ceased. King Kalakaua is credited with the revival of the *hula* in 1883 as a result of the colorful *hula* performances at his coronation. The dance revived during Kalakaua's time was the *hula kahiko*, the ancient style *hula* which is danced to vocal chanting and the beating of percussion instruments. The Merry Monarch Festival is an annual, statewide *hula* competition which celebrates the traditional dance.

Immigrants and sugar plantations. When land owners, who were primarily descendants of missionaries, established plantations on Hawaii, producing sugar for mainland consumption, another wave of immigrants arrived to be part of the labor force. Chinese laborers came in the 1850s, followed by people from Portugal, Japan, and the Philippines. The newcomers brought religious beliefs and customs from their homelands that have greatly influenced modern Hawaiian culture.

Queen Lili'uokalani, the last Hawaiian monarch. When King Kalakaua died in 1891 he was succeeded by his sister, Queen Lili'uokalani. She reigned for only two years, until the overthrow of the Hawaiian monarchy (see page 38). Like her brother, she attempted to preserve and promote Hawaiian culture. A natural musician, Queen Lili'uokalani composed many songs which are still loved in Hawaii today.

Haole. In Hawaiian, *haole* means foreigner or Westerner, particularly a white American. Many of the *haole* (often descended from missionaries) grew so rich and powerful through ownership of plantations and ranches and by becoming merchants and traders, that they took control of politics and government. A new constitution, passed in 1887, enabled the *haole*, even those without citizenship, to vote, while a majority of Hawaiians could not.

The revolution and the overthrow of the Hawaiian monarchy (1893). Queen Lili'uokalani was a strong ruler who wanted to regain control of the government and restore the rights of the native Hawaiians. But on January 17, 1893, a small group of businessmen, aided by the United States Marines, took over the Hawaiian government and overthrew the Hawaiian kingdom. The queen lost her throne. On July 4, 1894, the new leaders, led by Stanford Dole, formed the Republic of Hawaii.

Annexation (1898). On August 12, 1898 Hawaii lost its independence and became a territory of the United States. The Hawaiian flag was lowered, and the American flag raised over the 'Io-lani Palace. Once the residence of kings and queens, the palace was converted into the executive building and capitol of the territory of Hawaii. Annexation Day, observed in Hawaii every August 12th, commemorates this milestone in the history of Hawaii.

The pineapple industry. While the pineapple plant is native to the West Indies, Hawaii is known for the excellence of the fruit that it grows. Several early attempts to can pineapple in Hawaii failed because of the 35% import tax imposed by the United States. When Hawaii became a territory of the United States in 1898, this tariff was removed. James Dole, a young New Englander and a relative of Stanford Dole, came to Hawaii to seek his fortune. By trial and error, Dole began to raise pineapple successfully for the canning market. Pineapple canning, which had become the territory's second largest industry by 1920, resulted in a new influx of immigrants, including people from Puerto Rico, Korea, and the Philippines. In 1922, Dole purchased nearly the entire island of Lanai, making it the largest pineapple plantation in the world.

World War II. On the morning of December 7, 1941, Japan attacked the United States naval base at Pearl Harbor on Oahu. The lives of 2,335 U.S. servicemen and 68 civilians were lost; 188 planes and 18 major warships were destroyed, or heavily damaged. Immediately declaring war on Japan, the United States entered World War II.

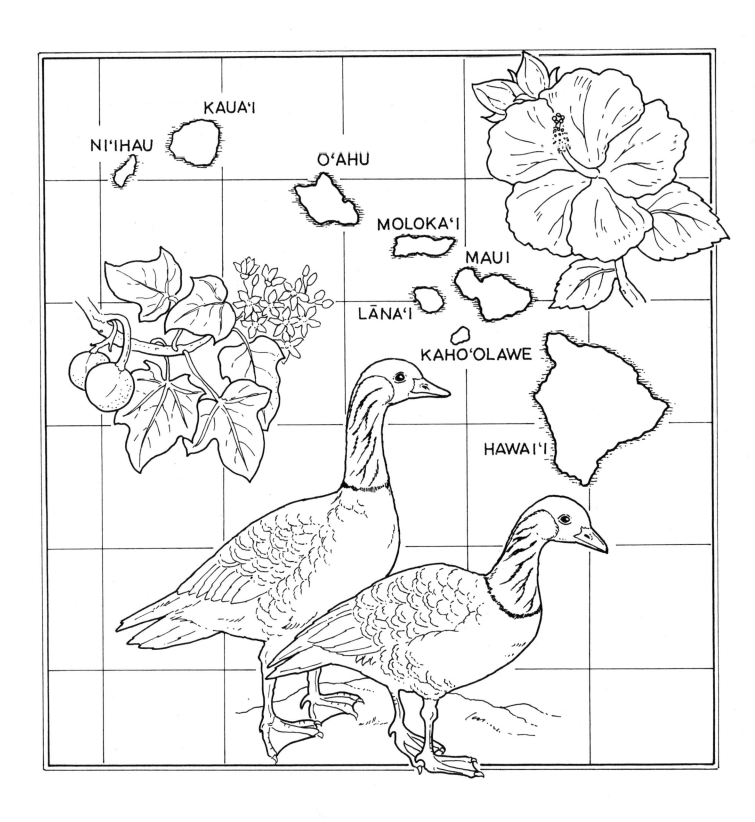

NI'IHAU
KAUA'I
O'AHU
MOLOKA'I
MAUI
LĀNA'I
KAHO'OLAWE
HAWAI'I

The 50th state. On August 21, 1959, Hawaii officially became the 50th state in the Union. Since then, its military stations and trading ports have become political and economic centers in the Pacific. Hibiscus is the official state flower, the candlenut is the state tree, and the rare Hawaiian goose is the state bird. As a group, the Hawaiian islands are called the "aloha state," but each major island has its own title as well. Hawaii, often referred to as the "big island," is also called the "orchid island"; Oahu is the "gathering place;" Maui is the "valley island"; Kauai is the "garden island"; Lanai is the "pineapple island"; Kahoolawe is the "uninhabited island"; Molokai is the "friendly island"; and Niihau is the "forbidden island."

"Hawaiian Renaissance." Since the 1970s, there has been a resurgence of interest in early Hawaiian culture. The "Hawaiian Renaissance," as it is called, has renewed Hawaiians' pride in their ancient heritage including the *hula* and its music, weaving and other crafts, language, and traditional agriculture. To better understand the remarkable navigational skills of ancient Polynesians from whom they are descended, Hawaiians have had a double hulled boat constructed. Called *Hōkū-le'a*, this vessel has traveled for the last 20 years between the Pacific islands. Since 1993, the 100th anniversary of the Queen's overthrow, the Hawaiian sovereignty movement has gained attention. A segment of Hawaiians are enthusiastic about the possibility of being internationally recognized as an independent country or being self-governing within the United States.

Leis. The custom of making and wearing *leis*, or flower wreaths, has been practiced by people in Hawaii since ancient times. In Hawaii, May Day (May 1) is *Lei* Day, a time when people wear *leis* and send them to family and friends as expressions of love and friendship. Many Hawaiians wear bright *mu'umu'u* dresses and *aloha* shirts as part of the celebration. The *lei* is the symbol of *aloha* which means "welcome" in Hawaiian. Each major island has a special island *lei*, and a special island color. Hawaii is red; Kauai is purple; Kahoolawe is gray; Maui is pink; Lanai is orange; Niihau is white, Molokai is green, and Oahu is yellow. Figure (1) a feather *lei*, (2) a shell *lei*, (3) a nut or seed *lei*, (4) *niho palaoa*, a necklace made from a whale tooth and human hair, worn by ancient Hawaiian royalty.

The Hula 'Auana and Hawaiian music. The modern *hula* is danced to melodies that are often a mix of Hawaiian and English.(See page 34 for the *Hula Kahiko,* the ancient style *hula.*) The modern *hula* is often accompanied by stringed instruments such as the *'ukulele* and the guitar. Adapted from a Portuguese instrument introduced in 1878, *'ukulele* means "leaping flea" in Hawaiian. The guitar was intro-duced by early whalers, traders, and Mexican cowboys. The stringed bass, mandolin, and violin are also part of the distinct Hawaiian sound. German bandmaster Heinrich Berger, known as the father of Hawaiian music, came to Hawaii at the invitation of King Kalakaua. Berger arranged more than 1,000 Hawaiian songs and composed 75 more.

Pā'ū. This Hawaiian female rider, draped in a colorful, graceful *pā'ū*, is a *pā'ū* rider. A garment that became popular in the 1880s, the *pā'ū* was designed to cover up and protect a rider's clothing as well as her dignity. Today, in the festival parades of Kamehameha Day or *Aloha* Week, each *pā'ū* rider wears flowers and a *pā'ū* in the colors of the island she represents.

Kamehameha Day, June 11. On this date, parades and festivities take place throughout the state to recognize and honor the memory of Kamehameha I. Hawaii's famous warrior king, he united the Hawaiian islands about 200 years ago. (See page 25.) As part of the celebration, the statue of Kamehameha I is draped with an 18-foot *lei*.

INDEX

(Hawaiian words are in *italics*)